Be The Beast You Are

Be The Beast You Are

AN APPROACH TO LIVING YOUR LIFE FULLY UNLEASHED

Shawn Antonio

© 2017 Shawn Antonio
All rights reserved.

ISBN-13: 9781548131029
ISBN-10: 1548131024
Library of Congress Control Number: 2017910357
CreateSpace Independent Publishing Platform
North Charleston, South Carolina

This is for everyone who wants more.

Introduction

What's inside of you and what do you want to unleash? What's stopping you? When are you truly going to use all of your potential in this lifetime? Why do you always wait for "**SOME DAY**" to unleash all that you are? It's now time for **YOU** to live the life you have always wanted to live, and **BE THE BEAST YOU ARE.** You have a chance to run faster than you've ever run, be bolder than you've ever been, be clearer than you ever thought possible. Be truly, fully you. We often pretend that what we want is impossible. But all you have to do is unlock all of your unique gifts and share them with the world. It's now time for you to create and design the life of your dreams. Today is that day.

Everyone has an inner beast just waiting to be awakened. You know how sometimes you get so inspired, you get so passionate, you get super clear about life? That's what I'm talking about. Awakening that beast and living solely in your own power. The beast is when you are at your best. The beast is your fire. The beast is your truth. The beast is always in you. You allow fear to get in the way of your beast coming out. Fear of judgment, fear of not being heard, fear of failure and even fear of success. You allow doubt and insecurity to stop your beast from showing itself.

What if you fed the beast instead? What if you actually operated from your beast all day, every day? How would your life look? Would your dreams be fulfilled? Would you create the life that you always wanted? I'd say yes. You wouldn't stop at anything and nothing would seem impossible. You can always have what you want – you just have to be bold and fearless enough to let your beast shine through.

Let's start by dealing with all the walls, borders and bullshit that you allow to get in the way of truly being yourself. You are going to look at all the different areas where you put all these things in place to stop you and keep you "right" about how life is.

We're going to look at:

- All of the outside circumstances that you allow to get in the way of you being your full beast
- The fears and white noise of your own creation
- How to feed your beast
- The actions that you are going to take to unleash your beast
- Keeping your beast alive at all times

Get ready to meet your beast.

CHAPTER 1
Letting Outside Circumstances Define You

In life, we tend to let outside circumstances get in our way daily. These circumstances are walls, borders and things we allow to distract us from our true purpose.

Take for example, a day where you wake up inspired to go to work and have a great day. You walk outside to your car and you have a flat tire. That circumstance could throw off your day, and usually you would allow it to. In that moment, you have a choice. To let that circumstance define how your day goes, or not. We, as humans will often let one thing that is an upset or a breakdown stop us from having that great day. We automatically take it negatively and make it a bad day.

We act like that circumstance can stop us from having what we want in life. It's a human reaction to something we perceive as negative. Something happens, we make it a negative and we give up. We all do this.

More often than not, you will justify the reaction from a past circumstance, so that you can define it and be right about how life is. When you're right, it keeps you safe and stops you from living the life you truly want. It's disempowering yourself and playing small. The opportunity you have in the moment is to handle the flat tire, move on, let it go and not let circumstance define your day. Fuck it.

So why do we allow such a small thing define our mood and way of being after the fact? Because it's easier. It's easier to get mad, blame the situation and have a shitty attitude. Life looks different every day, and we like to put things in boxes so it makes sense to us. That's the biggest problem – we don't look at these circumstances like a new experience.

We look at it like it's the same experience. We don't let go easily, we don't forgive, we're not free of 'what happened'. We punish ourselves because we feel guilty, we feel like an asshole, we feel like we're not good enough. We punish others because we don't want to be found out, we don't want to be seen as a fraud, we are afraid of judgment and being made fun of. All of that takes away from our true self, it steals fun, self expression and **ALIVENESS** from us. And life gets stale, stagnant and boring.

It's not that you're choosing to give up, or be in a bad mood it's just that you get stuck in the complaint of life and are used to carrying the complaint around. It's like garbage bags. We put all of our bad memories and bad instances in them and carry them around. And we pretend that we're ok. We load them up and we never throw them away.

It's not your fault. You've been conditioned by moments you have experienced in life. You are not actually consciously choosing to limit yourself, it's just a pattern that you picked up along the way.

We created those patterns in our early childhood. When we broke something, or lost something, or did something wrong and got punished. We learned what is good and what is bad. Then we learned to punish ourselves because of difficult experiences from our environment, our culture, our society, our upbringing. Family is usually the strongest of those influences.

When we punish ourselves, we cage our inner beast. Unfed, locked away and malnourished. We allow our self expression to die when we give power to a negative circumstance.

In that exact moment, you have the chance to define your way of **BEING** moving forward. You can be happy, you can be positive, you can grow or you can just smile and laugh it off. Imagine that you had that same flat tire and you saw it as an opportunity to learn how to change a tire. Instead of letting it ruin your day, what you get out of it is that you learned something new which makes you proud of yourself and you go on to have a great day.. This is an example of living true to your own power. This is what it means be the beast you are.

What areas of your life do you find yourself falling into negative patterns? Why do you set yourself up for failure?

Another thing that limits your true self expression is something I call "The Eggshell Theory". We start to live our lives based on avoiding being honest with ourselves and others, we avoid asking for what we want. The Eggshell Theory is when we are living trying to avoid upsetting the people in our lives. It's a learned behavior based on things that have happened to us previously. We try to avoid stepping on known landmines and triggers for fear of upsetting others. As a result, we are living withheld. We are not living fully unleashed and not allowing others to grow too. When you choose to live in your full capacity, the eggshells cease to exist. You're not holding back, you're just living your life.

Circumstances will always show up in life. It's all about how you deal with them.

When you step into your beast mode, circumstance no longer defines that moment, **YOU DO.**

CHAPTER 2
Human Noise, We All Have It

External things happen to us and then we subconsciously (and sometimes consciously) set up defense mechanisms or walls internally to survive life and keep us free from hurt and pain. We have to stop those patterns because they prevent us from living out loud. We have filters that cloud our vision as to what's right in front of us. Our filters are our safety net. To protect us from risking in life. We create fears from past failures, things people told us, our parents, friends, society, media and our culture.

The flat tire is a simple example of how external circumstances 'happen' to us. Now let's go deeper down the rabbit hole. Let's talk about one of my favorite topics – relationships. Relationships tend to be complex, because all people have their own set of external circumstances and internal filters that limit their full self expression. We let fear play a part in how we design our relationships. We aren't fully truthful, we don't open up, we only tell the best parts and not the ugly and we do this dance that doesn't make sense. We take these behaviors into our work relationships, our family relationships, our romantic relationships and our friendships. Your filters are a huge blockade, a safe haven, a familiar space to speak from. It's comfortable, it's easy – but also, predictable.

If you were just being you how would that go?

How would your relationships look? How honest would you be?

You wouldn't be afraid of just being yourself – you wouldn't be afraid of judgment. You would just be you.

Our Human Noise is that annoying little voice that we give power to. It says 'Do This, Don't Do That'. We do things out of obligation, out of guilt, out of 'have to' or out of 'should'. The truth in fact is, none of that matters. What matters is your ultimate happiness and staying true to your heart and gut. If you listen closely, your heart actually speaks to you. The white noise and fear is something we picked up along the way and it doesn't belong to us. None of that belongs to us.

Let's say you're going on a first date. On this first date, you have two options. To be fully you – open, honest and real or you can pretend, hide out and not be truthful. There is no in between.

You're on this date and all your fears show up. You don't believe you're good enough for this person. You believe that he/she is too hot for you. You have a story called "I'm not interesting enough" or "He/She isn't into Me" and you are slowly losing their attention because you are afraid and holding yourself back. So, what do you do in that moment?

You can keep pretending and the date is guaranteed to fail. No second date, no future. You are failing because you are not being true to yourself. You are failing because you are **TRYING** to impress the other person instead of just **BEING**. What shows up every time is your fears, your human noise and your walls and you shrink. When you let these things get in the way of your beast, you disempower yourself and you give up. You let fear win.

When you set a precedence of not being fully you, you not being the beast you are, you set yourself up for failure. Let's say for argument's sake, you do get the second date and end up in a relationship with this person. Now, this person doesn't really know who you are. You are holding back, almost like leading a double life. You are one way with friends and a different way with your partner. You end up frustrated and miserable and the other person feels shut out. This is all because your insecurities played a part in designing this relationship.

Alternatively, you go on this date and you don't allow your human noise or fears to get in the way. You walk in, you are honest about everything you are, you are open to the other person and you are fearless. You are truly free when you remove all your barriers and live in your true expression. This gives you the chance to truly connect. If you are being fully you, it gives the other person permission to be fully themselves too without fear or judgment. If you are both being authentic, you are giving yourself the best shot at creating something real.

When you remove your human noise and fears and live fearlessly, you can go after whatever you want without thinking. You can cast away doubt, uncertainty and just go get what life has for you. Now, the catch to that is you have to be honest with yourself in **KNOWING WHAT YOU WANT**. All these invented things are things we **CHOOSE** to put in the way to stop us. It's insanity, but we all do it. It's part of the human condition. It's not easy to push all this aside. It takes you looking at what stories limit you and where they started. Take the time to pinpoint those things and deal with them. Be compassionate with yourself. Be patient and love yourself. That's where it all starts.

CHAPTER 3
Feeding Your Beast

I know it's become popular to use the hashtag #beastmode. For each person, that means something different. For me, #beastmode means giving life all you've got. Using all your talents, gifts, ideas and energy. To be **UNSTOPPABLE**.

We often hear the term 'feeding your soul'. In this instance, feeding your soul is feeding your beast. Feeding your beast is simple.

Do things that nourish you and help you grow. Be passionate about your endeavors. Do that thing that scares the shit out of you.

How do you connect with **YOUR** beast? You connect with your beast by doing all the things that **SET YOUR SOUL ON FIRE**. That is where your beast lives. Breathing in life and taking nothing for granted. Simply stop fucking around and just be real with yourself. Remember the times you are **MOST LIT UP IN LIFE**? How did you get there? You did all the things that made **YOU** happy.

When you are passionate about something, all you can do is follow it, and feed it and live it. Passion is the fuel that feeds your beast. Insert passion into every aspect of your life and watch how life goes.

You need to get clear about what you want – and then you go after it. Don't put things in the way of your passion. Be unafraid. Be dauntless. Be on fire. That is the true way to feed your beast.

It's just waiting inside of you – it's waiting for permission. Stop blocking your passion. Stop being mediocre, being blah. You don't need to fit in. You need to be the best you that you can be. **YOU** have a unique set of gifts. What the fuck are you waiting for? Use them.

For example, I grew up around my mom, who was a scholarship Volleyball player. She taught me the basics of Volleyball. When I first learned, I was average with no ball control. I realized I had to practice. So, practice I did. Every day, I practiced my serve, my digs, my volley and I learned teamwork. Because I was passionate about Volleyball, I focused on being the best I could be. As a result, I became an amazing Volleyball player. We often distract ourselves and put things in place that don't allow us to focus on our inner passions. That's crazy.

It leaves us unhappy and unfulfilled. I say – let's break that pattern and only do things we are passionate about.

How would your life look then?

CHAPTER 4
Unleashing Your Beast

So now that you know where to find your beast and how to feed it – how do you live in it every day? When I wake up on a daily basis, I take a moment to look at my life. I then **DECIDE** and **DECLARE** who and what I am going to be that day. This is an active choice. When I give myself the power to be and do anything with my day, I empower myself to live freely. Living in that space, anything is possible. The way I live my life is simple. I wake up inspired because I'm alive. I wake up fully present to all the gifts in my life. Knowing that I have something unique to give to the world, and a difference to make. It is such a cool existence to go after and achieve the things you want. I love meeting great people and having great conversations. Not living on the surface. Life is all about moments, special ones that we create. It's up to us to be open, honest and real.

These are the choices I make daily. I challenge you to step into your own power.

I know that this isn't easy to do and can often be confronting. But that doesn't mean that it isn't attainable for you. You are the only one stopping yourself from being fully you. You are allowing your circumstances to dim your light. You forget how powerful you are.

Get out of your head.

I have already talked about how the only thing stopping you is you. Stop thinking about life and start doing life. I understand it can be uncomfortable – this is the human noise I talked about. The great part about living fully you is **FREEDOM**. This is living with your beast unleashed. When your beast is unleashed, you are fully alive. All that shitty fear doesn't get in your way. Living with your beast fully unleashed, doesn't mean fear won't show up. Fear is a part of the human experience. What it means is you now have the power to break through it. How much fun would that be – living a life not controlled by fear?

You are a unique being. You are a beast. Unleashing your beast is something only you can do. It's your gift to give to the world. When you hide out, you are cheating yourself, and the world, of the beast you are. That's selfish.

When you don't unleash your beast, life gets stagnant and is not likely to work out the way you had planned. You live in the impact of this and live a sad and unfulfilled existence. You are just surviving life, not living. You can explode when the frustration builds up. This is why being the best version of yourself is so important.

Here are some of my key actions to unleashing your beast daily.

- Love yourself. For exactly who you are.
- When you wake up, decide who you are going to be today.
- Be bold. Ask for what you want in life. Speak what's on your mind.
- Take actions despite fear. Be courageous.
- Don't wait. Stop procrastinating. Procrastination sucks.
- Lead with love.
- Do something out of the ordinary to break your patterns.
- Challenge yourself to be greater.
- Learn something new and apply it today.
- Do only things that make you happy.
- Cut the bullshit out of your life.
- Practice setting your boundaries. Honor them.
- Have real relationships. Be open and honest.
- Practice being unbroken. Remember who you truly are.
- Leave your luggage at the door.
- Trust yourself. Follow your gut, it won't steer you wrong.
- Don't waste time. Life is now.
- Never settle. For less than an extraordinary life.

You can take one or many of these actions on a daily basis to unleash your beast. These are just some of my suggestions on how to live fully self expressed. It is by no means a definitive list. You can write your own list of actions – what do you do to unleash your beast?

Try these out and see how life goes for you. I think you'll find that these will improve your life in ways you never thought of. It can help you grow and develop into the most awesome version of you.
IMAGINE THAT.

You can have a life that you have created confidently and on purpose. When you take action daily, you are in control.

When you take on these practices, it will take work. You have to consciously put these things in front of you. It won't be normal in the beginning to change your way of being. However, over time, you will become masterful and eventually these choices will be subconscious. You will have shifted and grown into your full beast. Living fully expressed will become normal. Watch out world, **HERE I COME!**

You know how you always talk about that **SOMEDAY**? Don't wait for someday. Make that **SOMEDAY** today.

CHAPTER 5
Living In Your Beast

In my experience of life, we fall out of practice in being extraordinary. Living in your new found power takes work. It takes effort. It takes work and effort because you become responsible for how your life goes. I truly believe that we, as humans, are actually afraid to have it all. The concept of having it all is scary. You actually have to get up and live fully each day. This is living in the beast. This is a daunting reality for most people. But isn't it fun to challenge yourself to just live freely? Isn't that what we all say that we want?

Then, here it is. This is your opportunity to **LIVE OUT LOUD**.

Living in the beast, for me, means keeping the fire burning. When I'm on fire, nothing stops me. I act fearlessly, I speak boldly, I have integrity and I am my true self. Simply explained, the beast is access to your true self. When I am being my full self, life is easy. There is no expectation, just doing. It doesn't mean that life won't throw challenges in your way – that is a part of your journey. What happens when you are in the practice of living in your beast, is that you handle it differently. Your perceptions are different. No matter what life throws at you, you can take it on with a new zest and bravado. It's up to you. It's always been up to you.

How do you keep this fire alive?

Let's start with negativity. You need to remove negative people and situations from your life. They serve no purpose and are toxic to your wellbeing and personal growth. I think we can all agree that we can easily identify things in our life that are toxic. We allow for it. When you remove these negative elements from your environment, you create space for positivity to show up. You'd be surprised at how quickly you can manifest good things when you cut the toxicity from your life. Practice identifying the red flags. There are always warning signs. Make positive changes and clean up your world. Don't allow outside influences to stop you from being truly you. You are the only you that exists. It's time to respect how special that is. Be you.

Living in your beast also requires you to be present. Focus on the here and now. Not the past, not the future – everything you need is right here. If you are living in the present, it is much easier to stay fully self expressed. You are not worried about anything else. You are just being. Now is all we have. This is how you stay connected to unleashing your beast and living it at all times.

Living in your beast requires daily practice. The practice is shifting your mentality and your thoughts. If you are creating from a place of whatever you want, per se, you can only naturally start to see changes because **YOU ARE DIFFERENT**. You are not doing the 'normal' or 'usual' way of things. Practice living in a space of being lit up by life. The more you do this, the easier it will become to subconsciously live fully in your beast every day. You choose every day how you are going to be. In order to maintain your 'fire' and increase your levels of satisfaction, you have to choose that path. Your freedom lies in the choices you make. When you choose something powerfully, it becomes who you are. You can then gain the mastery of your life. The shift in your mindset decides your way of being.

Think about when you take the time to be quiet and just **BE**. There is power and beauty in stillness. When you are still and present, you can actually hear people and you are not just waiting for your turn to talk. Most times in life, we are always waiting for our chance to speak instead of actually listening. When you listen to yourself, and others, there is clarity. I know for myself in recent years, I have struggled with 'just listening'. Now that I focus on listening, it gives me a deeper connection with others, and allows me to sit in my own power. That's where the gold is. When you are struggling to master living in your beast, practice being still and listening. It will quickly ground you and bring you present to your own awareness of self.

Being vulnerable gives you access to your beast. When you are vulnerable, ego and pride cannot constrain you. Vulnerability gives others permission to be vulnerable as well. Ego and pride are the biggest obstacles to living in your true self. When you step outside ego and pride, there are no limits to what is possible. As humans, we tend to shy away from vulnerability. We are afraid to let others in. There is so much strength in allowing those walls to crumble. To let others see who you really are. To share the deepest parts of yourself with others. This is the juice of life!

If necessary, you can set up reminders for yourself to take daily actions conducive with living in your full self expression. It may be helpful to do so until it becomes second nature to live in your beast at all times. What works for you? Take a look at your daily life and see what is missing to keep your beast alive. Maybe it's a physical reminder - an alarm, a note, a rubber band on your wrist. See where the triggers are that are most likely to push you into your usual ways of being. Is it just after lunch? Is it the phone calls with your parents? Is it when your boss comes to talk to you? Take note of where you naturally avoid being a beast. These are the places you hide out. Notice when you hide out, and why. This will give you access to your true power. Then, take those actions I discussed to unleash your beast. Don't get discouraged – it will take some practice!

Result

I hope this guide has given you access to a new world. One that has been living inside of you, waiting to come out. It's now your time to live freely and fully **UNLEASHED**. There is a new life, that is available to you and which you now have access to. Anyone can create it. Don't forget how powerful you are.

This takes courage. It takes work. It takes personal reflection and a willingness to go beyond what's comfortable. With these new tools, you possess the ability to define what's next for you. Without fear, self doubt, reasons or excuses. You can truly be the Beast you are. No more hiding, no more playing small. Just being.

Make sure to properly feed your beast daily. Follow your passions, ignite your fire. With a new mindset and a set of actions that give you extraordinary results. You can now live beyond what you thought was possible.

Be mindful of old habits showing up that allow you to slide backwards. Catch yourself before they grab a hold of you. How awesome is it to no longer be controlled by fear and outside circumstance?

Create the life you love.

You are in control. You choose how to be. This is where your beast lives.

Now you get to be the author of your own life. Live it.

Be The Beast You Are.

ABOUT THE AUTHOR

Born in Brooklyn, NY to immigrant parents from Panama & Aruba, Shawn Antonio was raised in New York, Panama and Florida. Shawn now resides in Los Angeles with his Australian wife and young family. A trained dancer, Shawn spent the early part of his career running a dance company after deciding that a degree in medicine was not for him. After relocating to Los Angeles in his early 20's, Shawn worked briefly in reality television casting before going on to become one of Hollywood's

Photo Credit: Josh Webb

most respected and well known event promoters for over 16 years. In that time, Shawn has met millions of people. His ability to remember people and places is unmatched. Shawn's enthusiasm for life and boundless happiness is electric and infectious. Shawn has always been passionate about advocating for people and has spent many years on his own self improvement and personal growth. Some of the people who have inspired him are Paolo Coelho, Mahatma Gandhi, Mark Twain, Albert Einstein, Dale Carnegie, David Bowie, Martin Luther King Jr. and many others who drew outside the lines and truly changed the world. Shawn has inspired and guided thousands of people in his life, and felt the time was right to start writing his own books. Shawn is passionate about photography and travel, and his favorite destination is Egypt. Shawn speaks fluent Spanish and English.

This is the first book in Shawn's "Finding Your Fire" Series. Look out for more titles coming soon.

Follow Shawn On Social Media!
@TheFireSeries
Facebook, Instagram, Twitter and Pinterest

ACKNOWLEDGMENTS

Wow, what a journey this has been, writing my first book. I have to say, it took digging deep within myself to create, share and open up my mind to what I wanted to write about. I have noticed lately that the world is in a tremendous amount of pain. I felt compelled to write this book now to help give guidance and expression to every single person out there. After all of the crazy conversations, amazing stories and poignant moments that have occurred over the past 5 years specifically, in my Heart, I knew that 2017 was the right time.

I want to start by thanking my Aussie Unicorn wife, Alicia Antonio. She. Is. Just. My. Everything! I have a saying I often use to refer to her. "She is like my oxygen. Without her, I can't BREATHE!" You know one of those people that changes the course of your destiny forever? She is that. The night we both met, we both weren't even suppose to be where we were. Then there is also this thing called "Kismet". She is my best friend, my sounding board, the one who holds me to account for who I truly am. THANK YOU and FUCK YEAH, BABE!! Life is just more FUN with you by my side. You will be the last face I see before I take my last breath.

To my resilient, unstoppable and warrior badass daughter Viva Jeanne, I am in debt to you. You have given me air, inspiration and power that wasn't possible before you joined us. Your spirit and tenacity for life along with your intolerance for less than what you want, has taught me so much. I often share my tattoo that says "Never Settle" with people to inspire them. Viva Jeanne, you are a living example of that and thanks for choosing me as your Dad in this lifetime. Now, let's have FUN!!

To my parents for being incredibly loving and supportive throughout this process and always being there for me. My mother Sislin has always been there for me no matter what. She is that woman. Nothing stops her spirit. My father Cecilio for simply being a great friend, which is awesome to be able to say about your father and just a badass man. MamaBear and Papa, THANK YOU. For everything you are in my life. Thank you for giving me life & guiding me with LOVE!

To my charming and beautiful sister Patrice Thomas, I simply SMILE when I think of you. I remember when you came into our lives. An afro of curly hair and an energy that lit up rooms, which you still have. I was the proudest big brother EVER on the day you were born. Since then, we grew up together. We had a lot of firsts that we both got to live through together. As they say, #PricelessMoments. I carry you in my heart daily.

To my rad brother Devon Johnson, You have always been my boy. When I say that, I mean, you came into my Life when I was 5 and as any brother would be, I was STOKED to meet you. We have had a crazy rollercoaster ride over the years and I absolutely LOVE YOU. You are one of a kind. Let's crush life together more often.

I am one of those people that remembers the impact of the people who have inspired me. I have so many to acknowledge & here we go. Thank you Tio Omar Albertto for taking in a 24 year old kid who came to LA to create a brand new life. Your generosity will never be forgotten. Thank you Suk Sung for taking me under your wing and reminding me I had my own pair of wings waiting to be used. Without you 2 Humans, I wouldn't have survived Hollywood. Claudia Klein, you have been screaming at me for years, " Shawn. Write That Book!". I finally listened. You're an Angel. My sister-in-law Kristin Hovell, you simply ROCK. Without you knowing, you taught me how to be patient, let people process life and give them space to step into their power. Before you, I got impatient at people for not living fully. Your feedback on my first draft gave me great direction. Mr. Daniel Andary, you my friend, have the gift of being engaged to Kristin Hovell and she too has the gift of you and your beautiful heart. Whilst you were here in LA, you challenged me in ways I needed. It helped me gain new perspectives on life and gave me the freedom to just let things be as they are. What a contribution. Kristin & Dan, THANK YOU BOTH for the MacBook which you purchased for us. You have given us the power to change the world. Lela Sky Woodward, your feedback and passion were unmatched and helped me take in the female perspective. Teresa De Gennaro, words kind of escape me when it comes to you. You are a light and presence that kept me focused as to why I needed to put pen to paper. Dennis Mulcahy, a.k.a. "Grandpa" a.k.a. "G-Pa", also known as my grandpa-in-law, You are truly special. You wowed me when I asked you about how you spent your 39th birthday by grabbing your journals and telling me exactly what you did that day. I have never witnessed anyone do that. Beautiful insanity. Thank you for cleaning up my grammar and helping me deliver this final product. To my mother-in-law Julie Hovell. You. Are. The. SHIT. It's the only way I can express how I feel about you. Thank you for taking me on that fateful walk in Flaggy where you questioned my intentions with your daughter. That day changed my life. Thank you for the 6 months I lived in Adelaide at "Casa De Viva" with you and spent priceless moments with you that are irreplaceable. Thanks for your contribution to this book and crossing out all of my curse words. Sorry, I'm keeping them. Ha. Thanks to my father-in-law Malcolm Hovell. Your spirit and pure LOVE for me from day 1 of meeting me warmed my heart. You immediately treated me as family and were also a fierce competitor on the bowling lanes. I'll take you on ANYTIME! I adore you and appreciate all the adventures we have had together.

To all of my dear friends out there who have been there for me, come to me for guidance, have shared their lives with me and held me up when I have fallen down, THANK YOU. This is off the top of my head in no order of importance. You ALL own real estate in my heart.

Armand Adamian. Stephen & Amina Pavelski. Adolfo & Kelian Suaya. Matthew & Angelica Gavin. Adam Calderas. Israel Gonzalez. Alen Aivazian. Matt Robb. Kristopher Forsythe. Tricia Bautista. Ian Eulian. Omar Johnson. Erik Johnson. Pat Johnson. Gema & Justin Cullen. Sage Gallon. Jeff Fong. Hayden Pacquing. Jackson Canning. Sara Bradley Matter. Amber Adcock. Julia Dyman. Barry Hoover. Jeff Luna. Brian "Flash" Mclemore. Tia Margarita. Matthew Dube. Blake Marshall. Terrell Davis. Glenda Williams. Adam Nello. Mollie Barrett. Sammy Albury. Sean Marshall. Sean Toohey. Janet Batchelder. Ira Kaganovsky. Ryan Sigman. Oz & Wendy Mejia. Kimberly Moreno. Mario Calderon. Anthony Montgomery & Vinessa Shaw. David Haley. Lauren Doty. Lindsey Doty. Mike & Trisha Bogdan. Shannon Martin. Smith Walker. Will Walker. Case McCone. Brad Hawkins. Retta. Craig Robinson. Adam Manacker. Maurice James. Mykel Owens. Darran Matthews. Zach Alpern. Mykel Tulloch. Cory Kirk. Eric Sorenson. Eddie Makabi. Richard Fields. Jen McKee. Ernest Skinner. Raul Martinez. Italia Nigro. Tim LeCoz. Vernon Gaines. Candice Moll. Steve Schlenitz. Betty Tran. Jana Oberdoerffer. Anita

SHAWN ANTONIO

Mohanessian. Christie D'Amore. Jason Dombrow. Lily Asinovsky. Morgan Gross. George Antonakos. Jill Olinsky. Lily Starr. Victor Togunde. Oscar Pinkard. Brian Williams. Manouschka Guerrier. Troy Thomas. Fabian Bates. Robert Ferguson. Rob Riley. Franz Latten. Sanyika Street. Jackie O'Neill. Dayna Williams-Hunter. Jazz Grant. Deep Sethi. Joni Lee. Marco & Marcello Cacioppo. Eric Hargrove & Nicole Faccuito. Michal Melamed & Todd Iorio. Reggie Watkins. Dennis Banks. Aaron & Ti Montgomery. Byron Hord. Ronaldo Richardson. Stevie Dupin. Kerri Watton. Julian Hovelle. Youssra Zehreldeen. Claire Paice. Brent & Jodie Petherick. Zac Raymond. Jan & Brett Tuckwell. Keithy Belding. Martina Stone. Sonya Giancola. George Ender & Angela Towne. Matthew Goldberg. Matthew Bello & Jannine Shirey. Hazel Angelino. Darrin Pfeiffer. Lamonica & Mina Garrett. Farhad Hajee. Wayne Chang. Joseph Hampel. Leyli Norouz. Kiara Belen. Ngai Barbero. Jessica Anderson. Adam Cleland. Stacey Wyatt. Frankie Jordan & Dion Mcinotsh. Ashleigh Nichols & Eddie Beasley. Obi Ako. Doug Miller. Erika Bryant & Chief. Todd McClain. Grace Hameister. Cody & Chelsea Jones. Vana Thiero. T.C. Carson. Jessica Bianco. Hailé D'alan. Sam Cain. Melissa Lauren. Sky Cole. Vanessa Caroline. Jarrett Levin. Carl Donelson. Mars Crain. Eric Todd. EJ & Victoria Hoyte. Vanessa Baclig. Life & Michelle Garland. LJ Mismas. Brandon Thomas. Jeremy Findel. Nava Cooper. Ben Cooper. Maya Plotsky. Kiki Cordero. Jennifer Dynof. Trevor Hansford. Christine Apa. Aaron Jennings. Kabir Sabherwal. Austin Wright. Tedd Money. Katie Darling. Alana Krigger. Shannon Haff. Raquel Blum. Rahsaan Mitchell. Mike Bitton. Josh Bitton. Rob Mersola. Jimmie Cervera. Daniel Lee Miller. Mariya & Froy De Platt. Khaled Shakta. Alex Luton. Craig Ley. Cristina Barker. Tamara Barton. Ed Lipnickas. Jill Blitz. Shola & Amber Richards. Sean Conley. Natalia Ludwig. Pat & Moses Dibenga. Annie Kasparian. Lindsay Brow. Bryon Schrekengost. Amy Phelan. Omar Alam. Yael Nucci. Christopher Ragle. Michelle Scarbrough. Rebekah & Tia Rimington. Simon Malak. Jane Paice. Leah & Vinny Dellay. Gustavo Flores. Ryan Ransom. Chris Snook. Sadie & Mike Dolan. John McNichol. Brett Hawkins. Ariyana Edmond. Chelsea Cahill. Fontaine J. Marsi. Kai Wanzer. Monique Stinston. Cara Brown. Ben Lee. Vueve Cross. Rita Stewart. Tess Polachek. Alden Kirkman. Caleb Alexander. Amelia & Brett Eagle. Omar Pierre. Stefan Stojkovic. Linda Andary. Christian Esposito. Cara Santana. Erlinda Vo. Nick Devars. Liz Angle. Law Jones. Jimmy Maslon. Cedric Valentine. Ti Woodward. Michael & Naz

Kade. Gerson & Juanita Horn. Landra Dulin. Mike Bareis. Mac. Rune Arden. Summer Altice. Ashley Greene. Steve Hart. Jimmy Franzo. Stephanie Clark. Marc Kreiner. Joy Brown. Tony Solano. PJ DeMarks. Whit Petrell. Cory Morales. Seven. Angela Salidas. Stephanie Rogers-Wells. Mark Manson. Eckhart Tolle. Hunter S. Thompson. Rumi. Ernest Hemingway. Don Miguel Ruiz. Mike Boogie. Meaty. Paris Paul. Nick Vodjdani. Ron Frierson. Simone Williams. Jonny Jonah. Michael Judah. Taurean Gordon. Matt Fite. Demetria Johnson. Alimi & Dahn Dior Ballard. David Ramirez. Mike Orlando. Ron Vitello. Anthony Hopkins. Evan Hembacher. Jensen Reed. Ben Goode. Howie Haber. Michael & Vicky Mirisch. Mac Africa. T-Pain. Dave Chappelle. Mario & Phil Soza. Zay Harding. Ed Anderson. Mobolaji Olambiwonnu. Mariam Frieg. James Feister. Matt Iott. Alex Boylon. Asa Gallagher. Ranai Maguire-Mahler. Deborah Maguire. Isabel Belloso. Blu & Laura Mitchell. Gregg Wadley. Jeff Keeping. Jordy Towers. Jeremy Schonwald. Stacy Theriault. Alex Gonzalez. Bernard Jacobs. Will Jackson. Jackie Melendez. Rachel Jackson. Gabriel Santiago. Greg Hancock. Dylan Caponi. Torrance Richardson. Chris Williams. Jeff Jacquet. Kat Valentina. Juan Martinez. Ashleigh Ethridge. Marty Sookasian. Danielle Burgio & Robert Merill. Paula Yoshikawa-Martinez. Auggie Del Rey & Brenda Sirena. Mike & Amy Piacentino. Robert Powell. Matt Greene. Anne Greene. Michael Anthony. Brent & Sonali Mata. James Pitts. Robert Figueroa. Devin Reeve. Awk. Pam Michelsen. Dane Flanigan. Michael McDevitt. Sammi Rotibi. Raquel Radlein. Shereen Roofian. Rebecca Dru. Jeff Parise. Danny Klein. Casey Keegan. Charlie Lew. Cain Vincent Dyer. August. Alando. Summer Raehm. Wade Belliston. Danny & Liv Blue. Adam Ambrose. Chris Cadenhead. Brian Watsabaugh. Jessica Quijano. Roger Steven Lewis. Freddy Behdinian. Cam Tangles. Benjamin Ross. Wil Figueroa. Woody. Eric Shepherd. Chad England. John Herzog. Ian Bohen. Kelly Reeves. Russ Greenspan. Chelsea Bass. Amy Moss. Jeremy Mclaughlin. Scotty Nicholson. Nickolas Potocic. Ray Berard & April Cate. Malcolm Ian Cross. Jessa Horowitz. Jennifer Lemus. Adam LeClair. Chris Cox. Galo Garcia. Elliot Cole. Garo Kilajian. Peter Kim. Craig Cordes. Kathryn Russ. Angel Manuel. Christian Bean. Robert Fagg. Alannah Skye. Nik & Vicky Mayer. Brad Weida. Jin Yu. David Quinones. Joaquin & Ashley Evans. Jay Jablonski. George Cardenas. Kim Gregory. Greg Richardson. Cleon Williams. Letitia Richardson. Michael Fox. Katina Cooke. Lisa Richardson. Sarah Spain. Reesha Archibald. Justin Brevoort.

SHAWN ANTONIO

Abu Kamara. Mary Duff. Emma Clark. Ramon Cartznes. Jennifer Page. Joe Ghanem. Amanda Canning. Tiffiny Walls. Amber D. Nelson Chiang. Jessica Davis. Toni White. Deborah Kennedy. Tom Barseghian. Blaney Barr. Noem Torossian & Team. Chris Robinson. Allen Davidoo. Clayton Canning. Jershi Lin. Shaden Tavakoli. Cia Kirchner. Kenzo Lee. Taylor Coles. Gregory Perris. Jim Mooneyham. Michael Moss. Angela De Silva. Connie Tripodi. Lenny Baskin. Juanita Baskin. Mat Yuriditsky. Henry Madatyan. Cristina Medina. Allen Nourhian. Danny Karam. Michelle Lee. Rachel Bajada. Kimberly Seitz. Andre Cotman. Lisa Einhorn-Gilder. Ben Jaimen. Jasmine Bates. Danina McKinnon. Dasha Voloshchuk. Krissy Lovecamp. A J Latham. Kirsten Humphries. Maitreya Yasuda. Quaye Kennerly. Tess O'Flaherty. Wesley & Jacqui Morris. Khadijah Karriem. Natasha Langhans. Jason Brown. Annabelle Riordan. Michelle Pesce. Ryan Bantu. Connie Parente. Sarah Maxwell. My Toca Madera Family. Le'John Smith. Jeremy McLaughlin. Gene Sun. Jillian White. Dylan Ben-Israel. Courtney Marie. Benin Harper. Rolando Gutierrez. Daniel Gutierrez. Serjan Markari. Max Martiri. Karl Mckinney. Sydney Hall. Travis Aaron Wade. JM Grimaldi. Mekyle Hussain Shojaie. Uzi & Vanessa Jan. Damian Love. "Still Bill". Simbi Hall. Unique. Derrell Span. Tony Marcum. John Bailey. Aron Mezo. Ezra Clark. Steve Kister. Garry G. Michael Rockstar. Rian Bosak. Phil X. Chris Jacobs. Ryan Christopher. Jason Paris. Michelle Conway. Kristin White. Keith Remington. Janeen Lowe. Shannon Malone. James Jones. Brett Kimball. Amir Ghany. Sarah Lynne Buchanan. Mohamed Moretta. Mili Matijevic. Mike DiFabio. Brian Raider. Tony Forde. Esther Cornett. Doug Phelps. Joey Vieira. Renee Deguara. Jeff Bomb. Chad Bordes. Jason Manacker. Dell Peters. Andrea Landis. B.J. Marjan Consari. Issiah Davis. Dena Skoko. Laura Calhoun. Andrea Wilson. Rob Stephenson. Mark Lentsch. Anita Mascioli. William Sculley. Emily Dean.

I also want to say that I have had the unique gift and pleasure of meeting thousands and thousands of people over my lifetime and if I didn't mention you, I apologize. Please know that you're in my heart. I have tons of room in there.

In closing, I love and adore you ALL and thanks for breathing life into this book. This is the beginning of a long and beautiful journey together. You are now responsible for changing many, many lives. Deal with it.

Made in the USA
Middletown, DE
29 February 2020